Roots of Rhythm

The purpose of this book is to explore the basics of drumming. The goal is to train the mind to separate from the body, using sticking patterns and repetition. The exercises require only a pair of sticks and patience to learn the fundamentals of performing the drums, although a metronome is highly recommended and necessary at times for improving. Most of what I play today I learned from taking private lessons, high school jazz band, and playing with friends often.

Although geared for beginners, the exercises in this book are ones that I practice regularly. I have designed exercises in this book the way I approach new rudiments. The study of any musical instrument is a lifelong journey. There is always more to learn and it is ever evolving. I recommend any and every avenue that brings one closer to music, be it school band, private lessons, online videos, live performances, etc. The more time and thought you put into music and musical concepts, the more you will develop and become more comfortable.

Play everything straight and on time. I strongly recommend practicing everything to a metronome. The concepts in this book are fundamental to playing more complex things, so spend plenty of time learning them.

– Robert Grubaugh

TABLE OF CONTENTS

POSTURE

Up Hand Position

This is the "**up**" position, or stroke, of the German grip. The palms face down and the fingers are loose and relaxed, waiting to catch the stick after the rebound of the downstroke.

Down Hand Position

This is the "**down**" position, or stroke, of the German grip. Keep arm, wrist, and finger muscles pretty relaxed.

FUNDAMENTALS

Counting

Rudiments make up most of what you play on the drum set. They are note groupings played in different sticking patterns that create rhythms. A beat, sometimes called a groove, is a repetitive pattern played on the drum set. It determines the tempo or pulse of the song, measured in BPM, or beats per minute. The pulse is counted, usually in quarter notes, as follows; **1, 2, 3, 4.** You could count eighth notes as well; **1 and, 2 and, 3 and, 4 and,** making eight notes per bar. This is helpful when playing 16th notes. Counting sixteenths; **1 e and a 2 e and a 3 e and a 4 e and a...**

Count out loud and try to internalize counting while moving your limbs. The more you practice to a metronome the more this will all make sense. **Fills** are patterns of note groupings. **Drum rolls** are a common fill that are generally played faster than the beat thus emphasizing a change in the music and feel of the song. Take plenty of time on all of the rudiments in this book. Play them slow to fast, and backwards. For rudiments like the **paradiddle** (found on page 10), try mixing up the pattern in whatever way is fun. The point of practicing rudiments is to build strength and coordination. It's possible to explore combinations of rudiments and different ways to subdivide rudiments to create tension or release.

Definitions & Music Notation

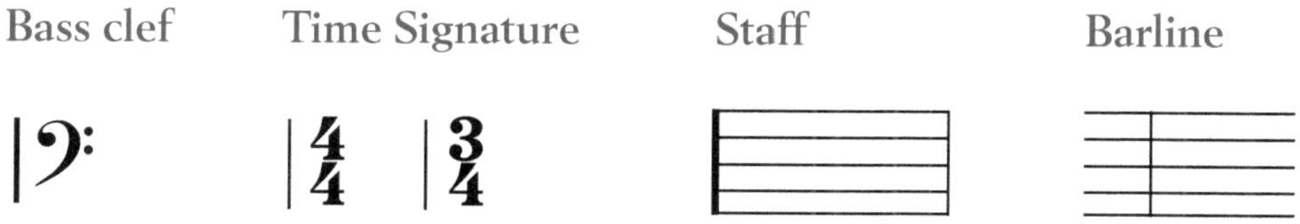

Bass clef
Time Signature
Staff
Barline

Tempo

Beats Per Minute (BPM)
for example, **92 BPM**

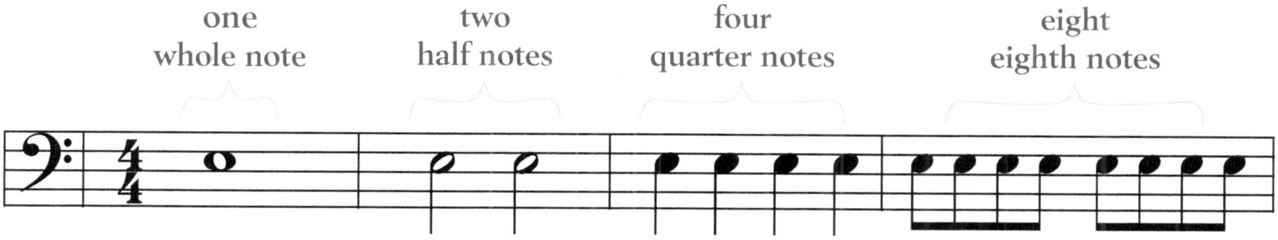

one whole note
two half notes
four quarter notes
eight eighth notes

Measures: consist of a given amount of notes according to the time signature. 4/4 time is **four quarter notes** within a measure. You can see the **eight eighth notes** in the last measure above, but you can continue subdividing to 16th notes, 32nds, and 64ths. It's all about how many notes you a want to play within a measure that creates interest within the music.

WARM UP

Warming up is important before playing. It's also a good way to simplify your playing and get used to how the sticks feel in your hands. Focus on keeping your wrists relaxed and allow the sticks to find a natural position in which they bounce easily.

These exercises are good for learning how to hold the sticks as well as warm up the hands and arms, preventing injury when playing for longer amounts of time.

R - Right hand   L - Left hand

RUDIMENT 1
Single Stroke Roll

The first rudiment is a **single stroke roll**. It's called a single stroke because each hand strikes the drum head once in succession. The pattern repeats making a drum roll. Play as evenly and with the same force in each hand as possible. Start with both sticks about **18 inches** off the drum head. Start slow and build speed, focusing on playing with steady and even force, then playing at different tempos to a metronome.

◆ The goal is not to play fast! Speed only comes with plenty of time and practice.

R L R L   R L R L   R L R L   R L R L

L R L R   L R L R   L R L R   L R L R

◇ Eighth notes

R L R L R L R L   R L R L R L R L   R L R L R L R L

L R L R L R L R   L R L R L R L R   L R L R L R L R

RUDIMENT 2
Double Stroke Roll

The second rudiment is a **double stroke roll**. Each hand strikes the drum twice in succession. Think of it as doubling a single stroke roll. Instead of **R L R L**, for a single stroke roll, the sticking for a double stroke roll is **R R L L**. The double stroke roll is a great rudiment to master. Play every stroke evenly and with the same force.

R R L L   R R L L   R R L L   R R L L

L L R R   L L R R   L L R R   L L R R   L L R R   L L R R

◇ **Variations**

R L L R   R L L R   R L L R   R L L R

L R R L   L R R L   L R R L   L R R L   L R R L   L R R L

RUDIMENT 3
Paradiddle

The third rudiment is a **paradiddle.** It's a very common rudiment in many genres. It works well in 1/16th note grooves and for fills. Take time with this rudiment and try it in all kinds of different sticking patterns. The traditional paradiddle is **R L R R L R L L.** Many drummers put the double stroke at the beginning or in the middle giving the rudiment a different feel. Drums are all about inventing and moving patterns around within bar lines.

◆ Go **SLOW** and make sure the double stroke isn't being bounced when played slow. You want every stroke to sound the same!

R L R R   L R L L   R L R R   L R L L

L R L L R L R R   L R L L R L R R   L R L L R L R R

R R L R   L L R L   R R L R   L L R R

L R R L R L L R   L R R L R L L R   L R R L R L L R

RUDIMENT 4
Flam

The fourth rudiment is a **flam**. Flams are a **ghost note**, or a note played quietly, struck just before the note that's on beat. Unlike all the other rudiments in this book, one hand will play the flam much softer to get the effect. Flams can be added to any rudiment to create more complex fills or rolls. For the sticking, the flam will be represented by a lower case "**r**" or "**l**". Instead of keeping the sticks 14 to 18 inches above the drum or pad, keep one hand between **2 and 6 inches** away. Flams are great for groupings of 3's.

rL R L R   lR L R L   rL R L R   lR L R L

rL R L L lR L R R   rL R L L lR L R R   rL R L L lR L R R

r L L L   l R R R   r L L L   l R R R

◇ **Triplets!**

3   3   3   3

r L L R l R R L   r L L R l R R L

7

EXERCISES

Repeat each exercise 30 times in a row smoothly, at the same volume for every hit before moving on to the next exercise.

Go **SLOW** and count out loud in time with a metronome; **1   2   3   4**

- When things get comfortable and become second nature, try starting on the second beat of the measure.

1

R L R L   R R L L   R L R L   R R L L   R R L L   R R L L

2

L R L R   L L R R   L R L R   L L R R   R R L L   R R L L

3

R L R R   L R L L   L L R R   L L R R   R L R R   L R L L

4

L R L L   R R L R   L R L L   L L R R   L L R R   L L R R

5

L R L R   L L R R   L R L R   L L R R   L R L R   L L R R

6   RLLR LLLL   RLLR LLLL   RLRR LRLL

7   LRRL RRRR   LRRL RRRR   LRLL RLRR

8   RLRR LLRL   RRLL RLRR   LLRL RRLL

9   LRLL RRLR   LLRR LRLL   RRLR LLRR

10 RRRL LLRR   RLLL RRRL   LLRR RLLL

11 LLLR RRLL   LRRR LLLR   RRLL LRRR

12 LRLR LLRR   LRLR LLRR   LLRR LLRR

9

13 — L R L L   R R L R   L L R R   L R L L   R R L R   L R L L

14 — R L R R   L L R L   R R L L   R L R R   L L R L   R L R R

15 — L L R R   L R L L   R R L L   R L R R   L L R R   L R L L

16 — R R L L   R L R R   L L R R   L R L L   R R L L   R R L L

17 — R R R L   L L R R   R L L L   R R R L   L R L L   R R L L

18 — L L L R   R R L L   L R R R   L L L R   R L R R   L R L L

19 — R R R R   L L L L   R R R R   L L L L   R R R R   L L L L

10

20
R L R L R L R R L R L R L R L L R L R R L R L L

21
L R L R L R L L R L R L R L R R L R L L R L R R

22
R L R R L L L R R R L R L L L R R L R R L R L L

23
L L R R L R L R L L R R L R L L L L R R L R L R

24
R R L L R L R L R R L L R L R R R R L L R L R L

25
R L R R L R R R L R L L R L L L R L R L R R L L

26
L R L L R L L L R L R R L R R R L R L R L L R R

— STAFF PAPER —
Create Your Own Exercises

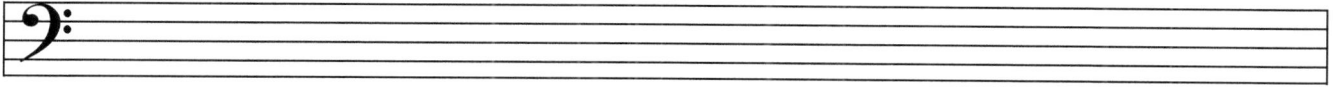

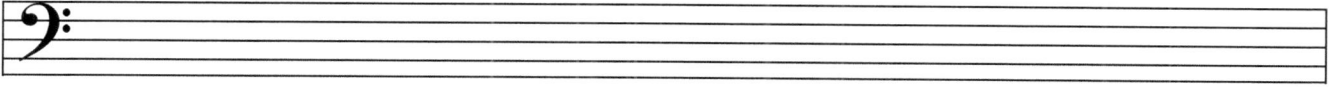

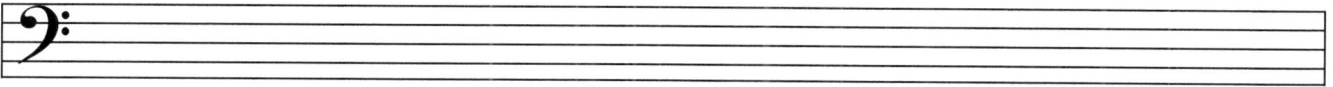

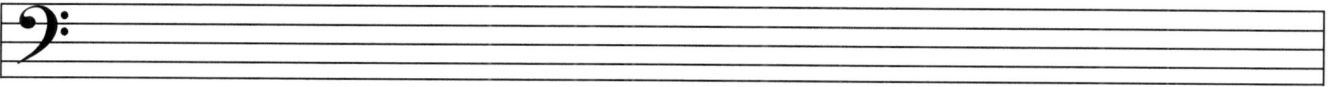

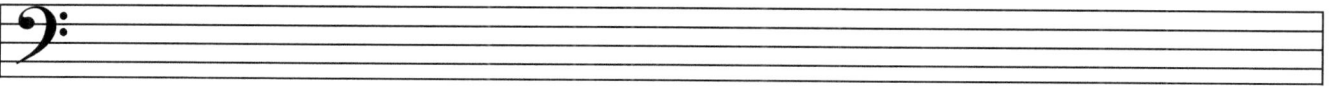

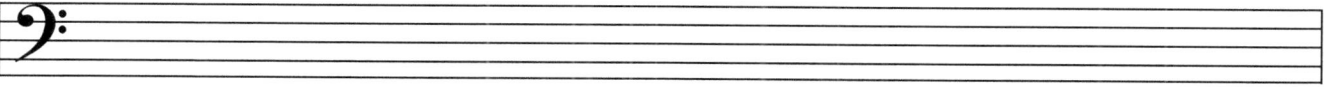

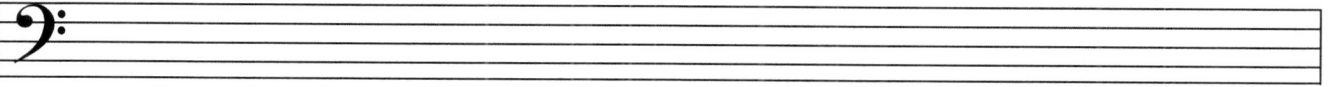

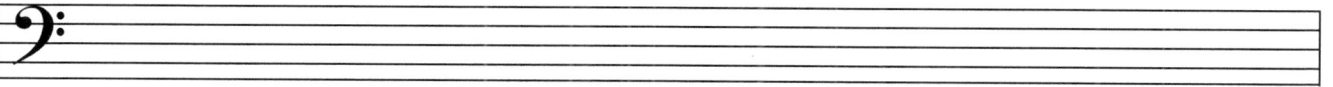

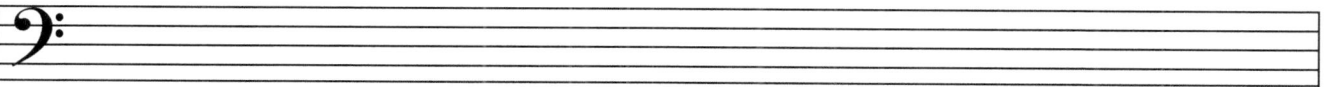

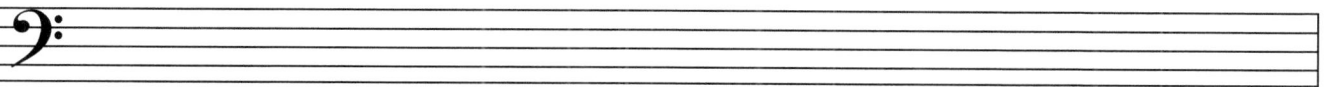

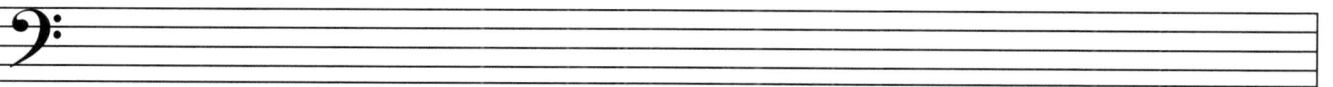

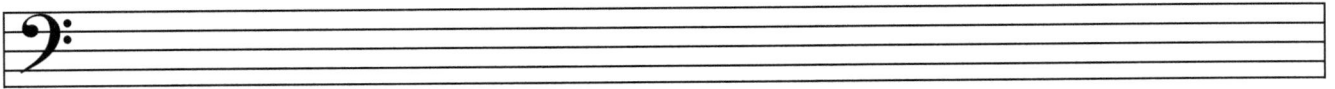

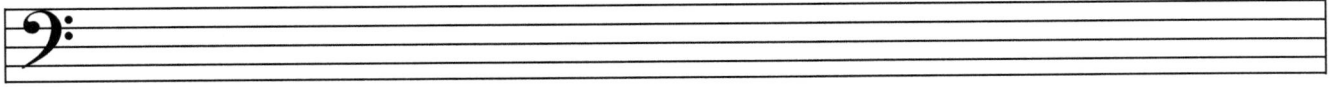

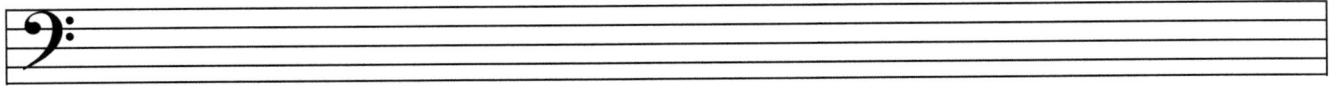

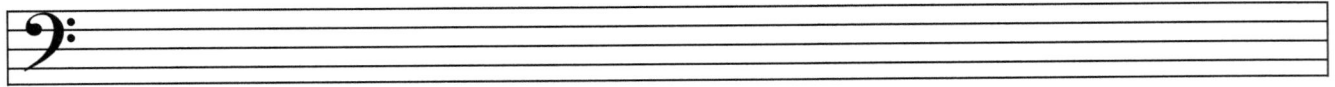

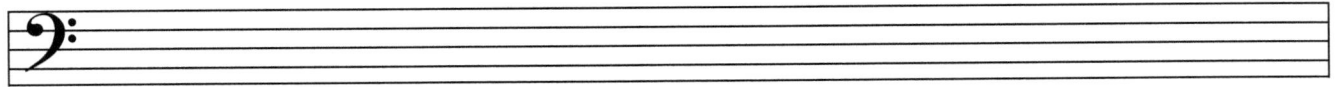

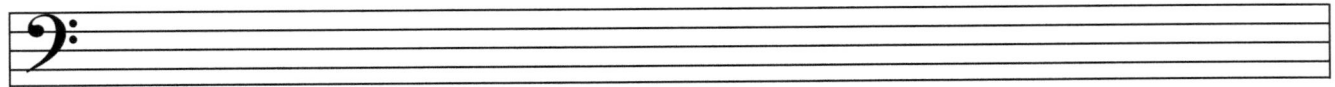

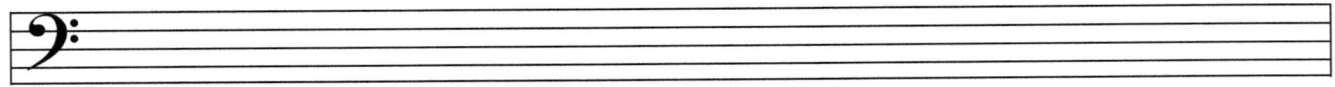

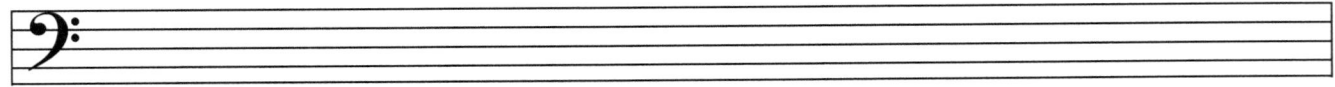

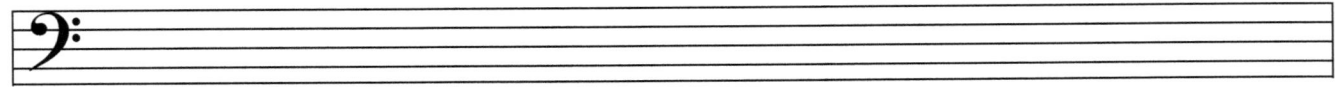

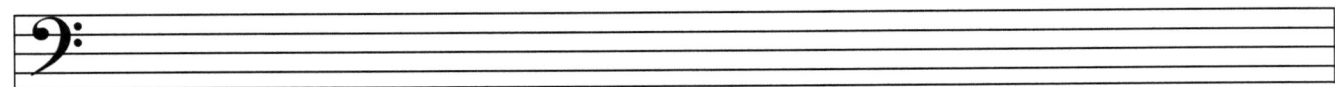

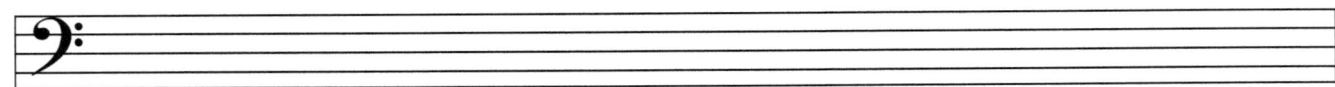

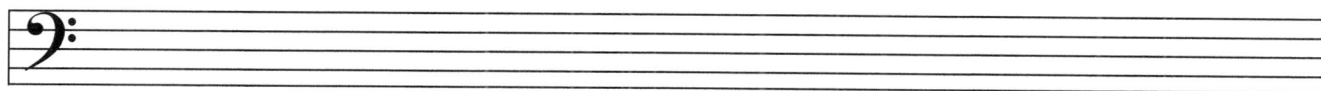

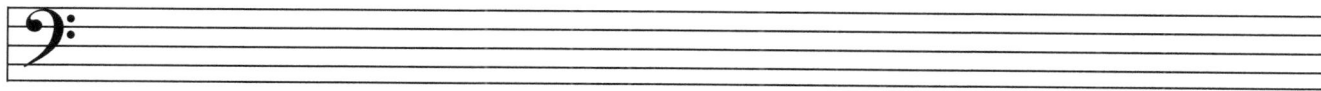

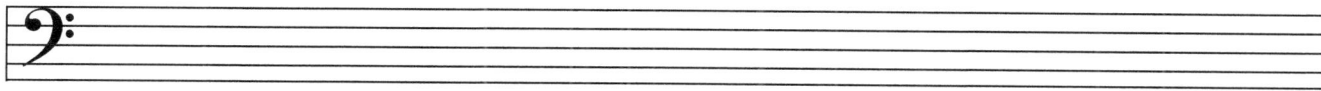

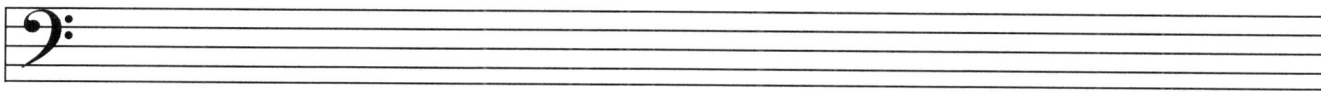

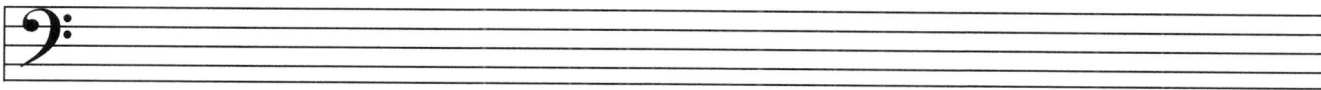

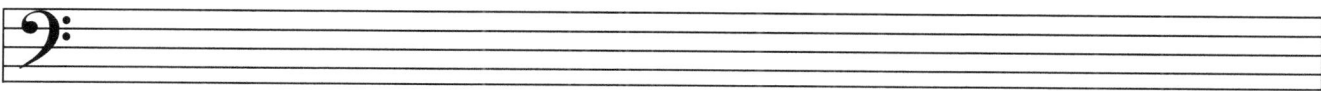

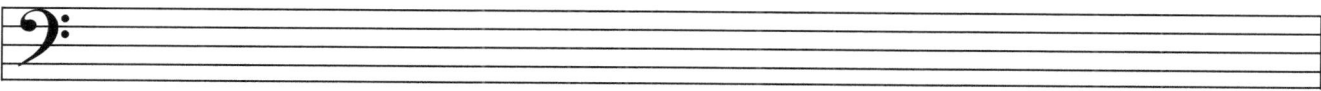

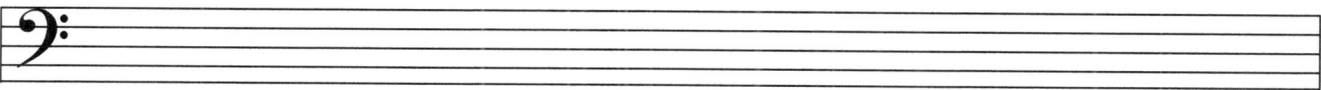

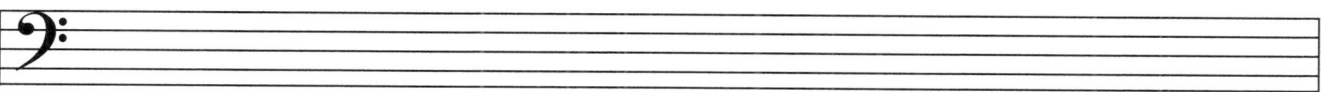

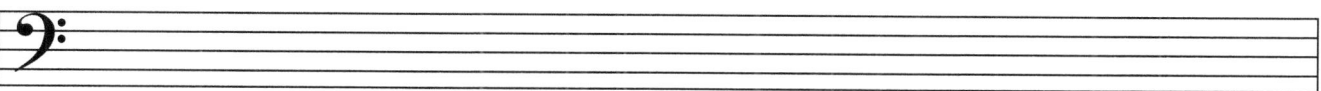

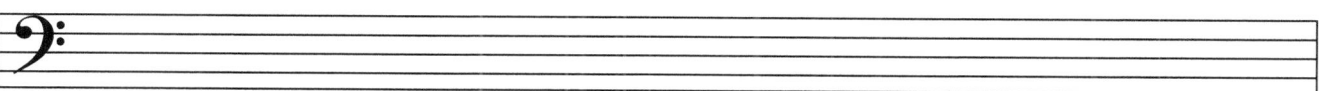

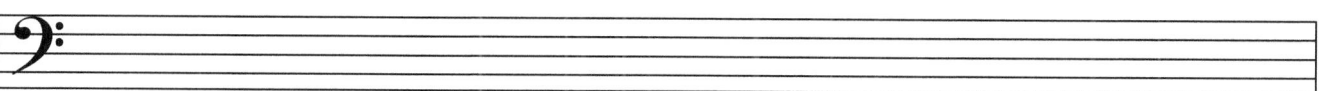

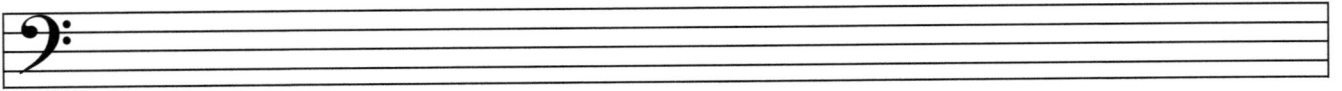

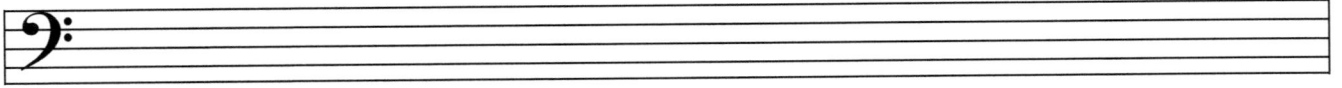

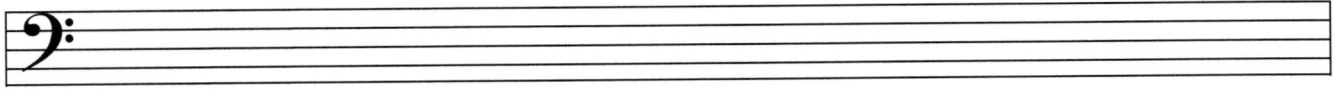

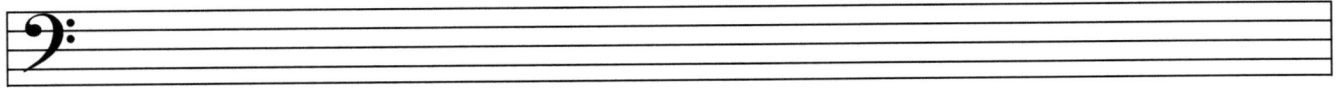

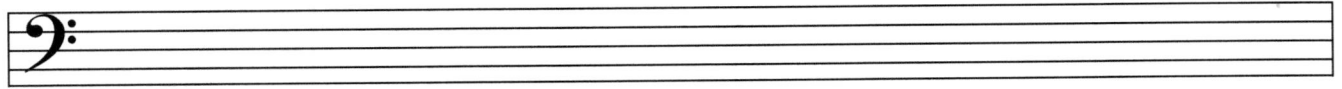

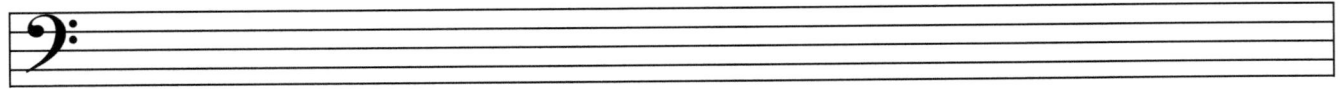

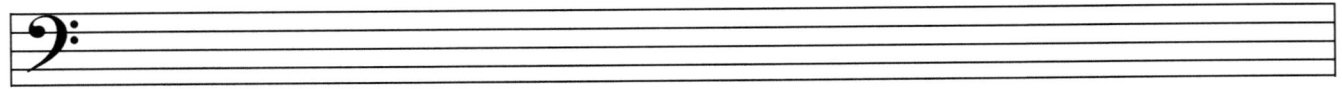

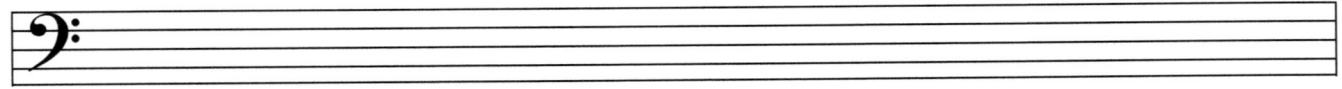

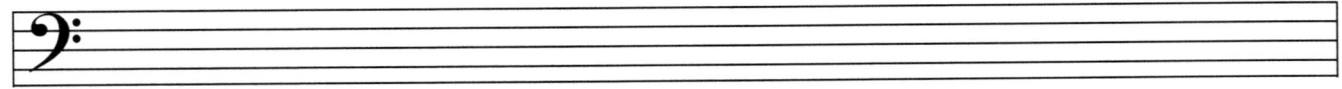

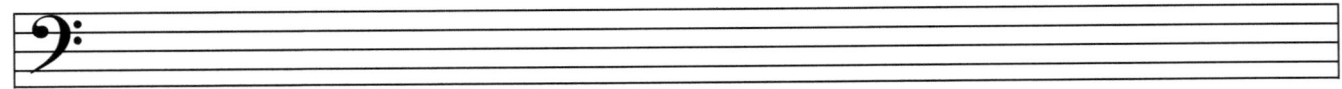

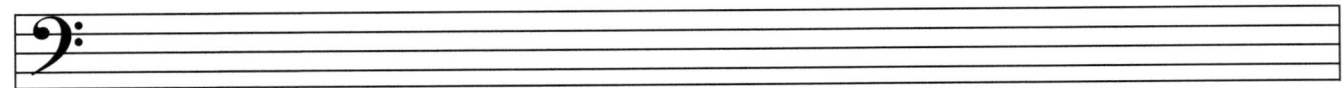

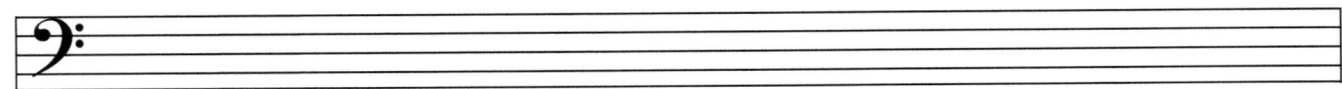

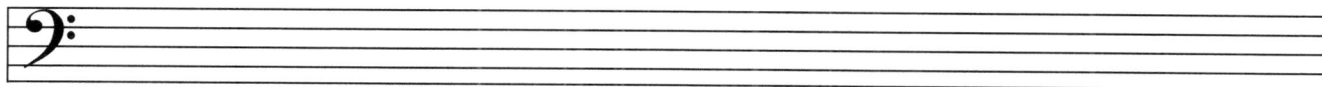

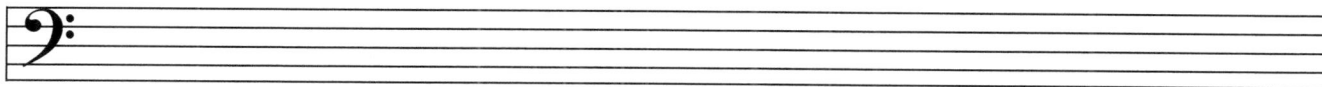

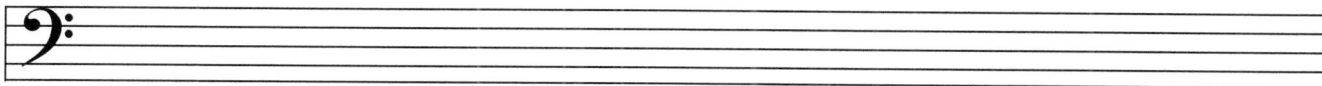

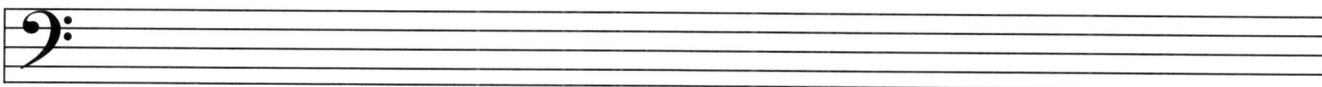

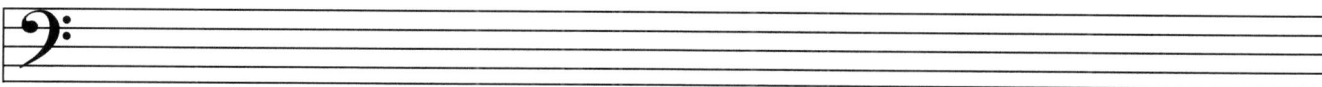

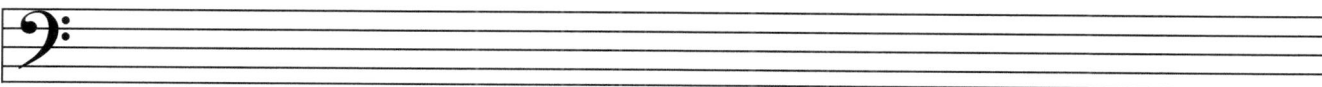

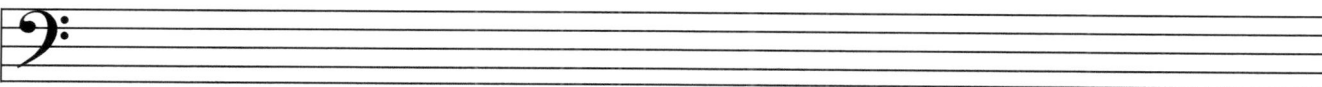

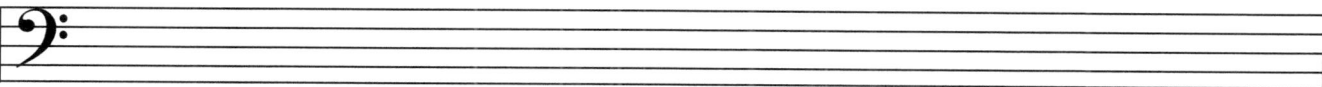

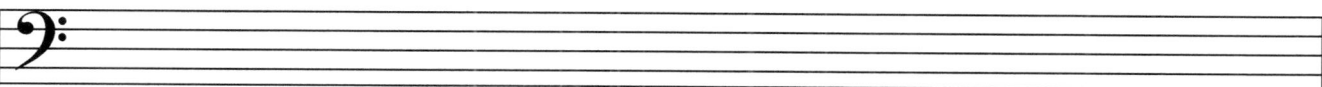

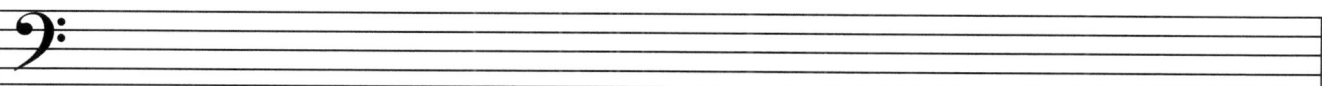

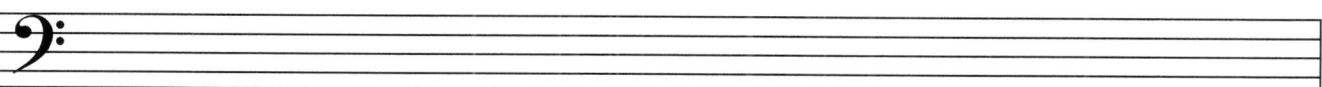

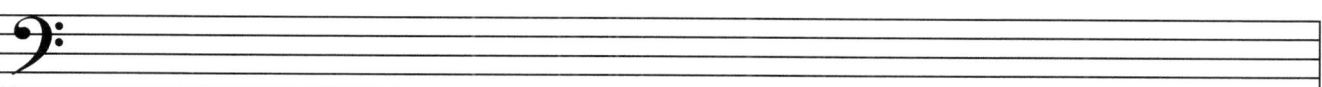

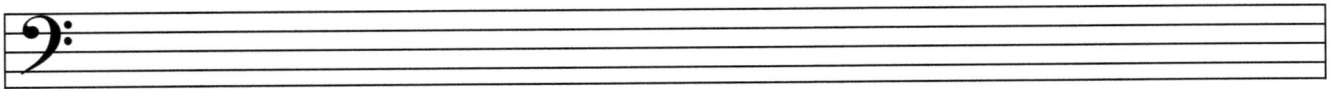

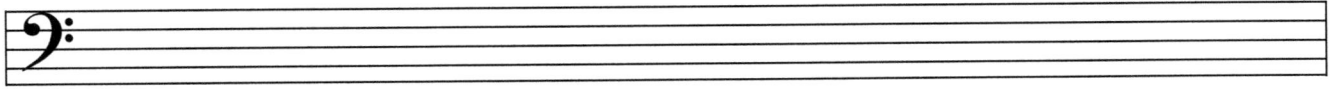

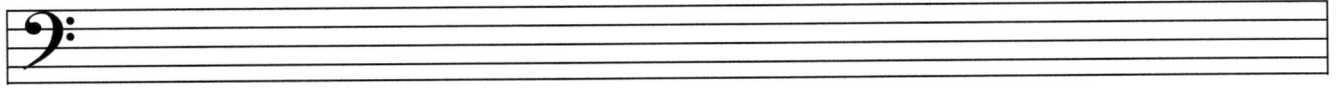

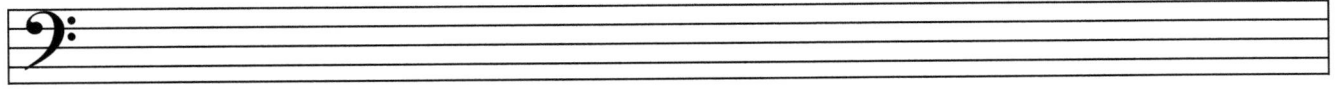

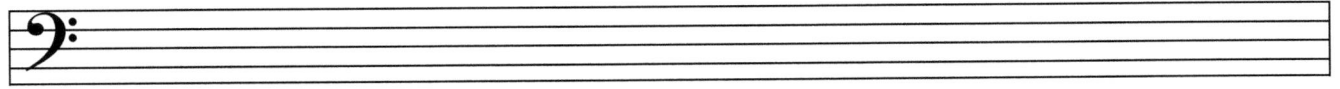

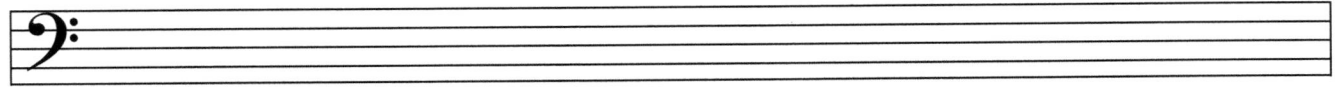

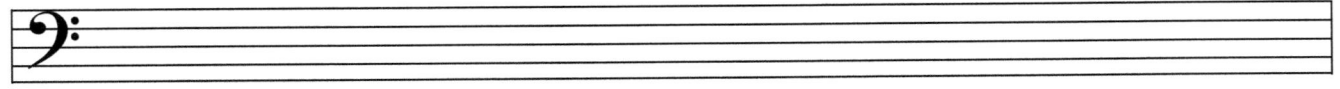

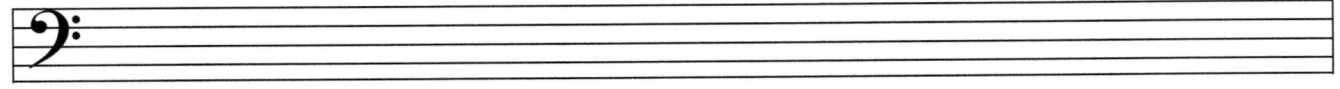

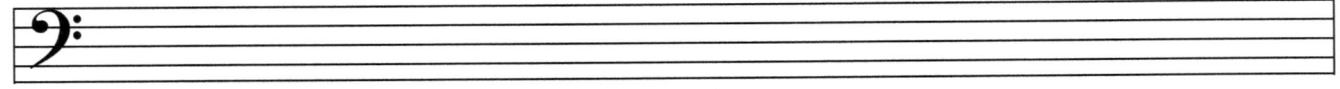

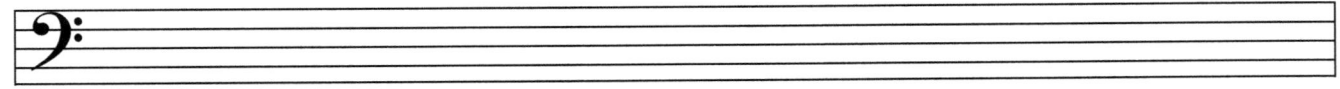

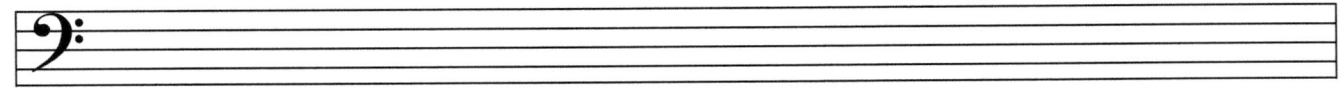

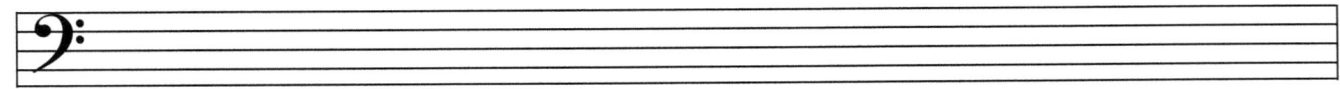